DATE DUE			

WE CAN SAVE THE EARTH

THE ANIMALS WE LIVE WITH

Written by:
Jill Wheeler

Published by Abdo & Daughters, 6535 Cecilia Circle, Edina, Minnesota 55439

Library bound edition distributed by Rockbottom Books, Pentagon Tower, P.O. Box 36036, Minneapolis, Minnesota 55435

Library of Congress Number: 90-083604   ISBN: 1-56239-005-8

Cover Illustrated by: C.A. Nobens
Interiors by: Kristi Schaeppi

Edited by: Stuart Kallen

TABLE OF CONTENTS

INTRODUCTION

A huge dinosaur walks across the grasslands. Bending down, the dinosaur rips a small tree out of the ground and chews it. Smaller animals run in terror as the dinosaur munches the tree.

Once, millions of dinosaurs roamed the earth. One by one, they died out. When every one of a certain kind of animal dies, we say the animal is *extinct*. Dinosaurs became extinct millions of years before human beings lived on the earth.

It's hard to imagine a world where animals are extinct. Animals affect us every day. Some animals provide us with food and clothing. Others entertain us with their songs, their beauty and their activities. Still others make our world more enjoyable through their companionship. Our lives would be very different without animals. In fact, human beings could not live without other animals.

There are many animals today that are in danger of becoming extinct. Take large cats, for example. There are many different kinds of large cats, including leopards, lions, jaguars, cheetahs and tigers. The snow leopard is just one *species* of large cat. There are very few snow leopards left today. Soon there may no longer be any snow leopards in the world. Because they are in danger of dying out, we say snow leopards are an *endangered* species.

When an animal becomes extinct, we all lose. We lose the joy of watching them. We lose the resources they can provide us. Worst of all, the animals suffer as they die, one by one.

Many kinds of animals already have vanished from the face of the earth. Others are in danger of disappearing forever. But there is still time to save some of them if everyone works together.

This book describes some extinct animals. It also tells about endangered species and what each of us can do to save these animals. Think about how important animals are to you, and ask your friends to do the same. Then get busy before time runs out, and the animals are gone forever.

CHAPTER 1
Dinosaurs and Dodos
A History of Extinction

Extinction can be part of nature. As you read earlier, dinosaurs roamed the earth millions of years ago, but these giant lizards became extinct because their bodies could not adapt to the changing climate and vegetation.

Other prehistoric animals, such as the woolly mammoth and the saber-toothed tiger, also became extinct because they could not adapt. These animals became extinct because of some change in nature. A change in weather or food can cause natural extinction. There were humans on earth when these animals lived, but people probably did not cause these animals to become extinct.

A big difference between natural extinction and extinction caused by humans is that natural extinction can take millions of years. People can cause an animal to become extinct in only a few years.

How can this happen? People can make animals extinct in many ways. One way is by killing animals faster than they can reproduce. This happened with a bird called the passenger pigeon.

At one time, billions of passenger pigeons lived in North America. The sky became dark when these huge flocks of birds flew overhead.

During the 1800's, pioneers began cutting down the forests where the birds lived. They also discovered that the birds were good to eat, so they began to hunt them. They killed so many of them so quickly that the birds could not hatch and raise their young. The very last passenger pigeon died in a zoo in 1914.

Other times, humans cause animals to become extinct by changing the enviroment, or *habitat*, in which the animals live. The dodo bird was a large, flightless bird that lived on the island of Mauritius in the Indian Ocean. The bird was slow and could not defend itself. The dodo survived on the island because no other animals hunted it there.

The situation changed in the 1600's when humans settled on the island. They brought with them dogs, cats, and other animals that chased, caught and ate the dodos. The animals also ate the dodos' eggs. All the dodos were dead by 1800.

The dodo and the passenger pigeon are just two examples of animals that have become extinct in recent history. Because of people, more than 100 species of mammals and birds have vanished forever in the past 300 years.

Extinction is not just a problem of the past. It is even worse today. About 10 percent of all species of life on earth are endangered. That rate is increasing rapidly. In the next chapter, you'll find out what humans are doing to cause this problem.

Passenger Pigeon and Dodo Bird.

CHAPTER 2
Endangered Animals

As you have seen, people make animals extinct by killing too many of them for food, or by changing an animal's habitat so the animal no longer can survive. There are many other ways people hurt animals. The following reasons are some ways people cause species to become endangered today:

Species become endangered because people kill them for money. Crocodiles are endangered because people have killed so many of them for their skins. Elephants are endangered because people are killing them for their ivory tusks. When people stop buying things made from ivory and crocodile skins, there will be little reason for people to kill these creatures.

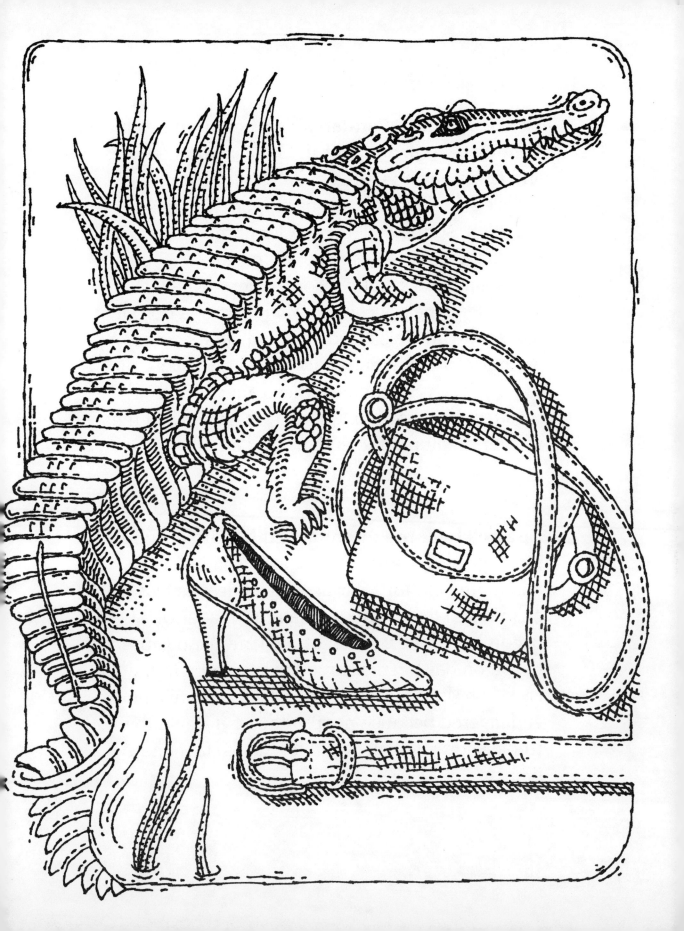

Species become endangered because people believe they are harmful. Grizzly bears, wolves and tigers have become endangered. People believe these animals are harmful to humans or livestock, so they kill them. Often, the animals are not dangerous, they simply are misunderstood. For example, farmers become angry when wild animals kill their livestock. Many farmers do not realize the animals are only doing what comes naturally to them, and that wild animals were on the land first. Sometimes, these animals kill livestock because human hunters have killed the smaller creatures the endangered animals normally eat.

Species become endangered because people take up more land. People are claiming more and more land for their use, which leaves less for animals. China's giant panda is in danger of becoming extinct. Much of the land pandas used to live on has been cleared for farming. On the island of Madagascar, many species of animals are endangered because people have cut down the tropical forests they live in for crops, fuel and timber.

14

Species become endangered because people want them as pets. There are only about 300 woolly spider monkeys left in the world today. There are two reasons these monkeys are in danger of becoming extinct. Their rainforest homes are being destroyed and people trap them and sell them as pets. If people refuse to buy woolly spider monkeys for pets, the monkeys will have a better chance of survival.

Species become endangered because people pollute the environment. The beautiful peregrine falcon is on the endangered species list because of DDT, a poison used to kill insects on crops. The poison built up in the bodies of birds that ate insects killed by DDT. Peregrine falcons then ate these poisoned birds. The chemical caused the falcons' eggs to have very thin shells, so the shells broke and the baby falcons died.

Some people are not being good neighbors to the animals we live with. We need to remember that animals have a right to share the earth with us. They deserve our love and respect. It is wrong to kill endangered animals simply to make money. And it is wrong to cut down forests without thinking about how it will affect the animals that live there.

CHAPTER 3

Why Should We Care About Endangered Animals?

Most people agree that it is wrong to make an animal species extinct. But there are other reasons why we should care about the fate of endangered species.

Every living thing, or *organism*, on earth is part of what is called an *ecosystem*. An ecosystem is the web of plants, animals and other natural elements surrounding an organism. Everything that happens to any member of the ecosystem has an effect on other members.

Did You Know . . .

A pine cone stuffed with peanut butter is a good way to feed birds during the winter.

Did You Know . . .

Growing wildflowers will provide food for beneficial insects.

For example, in the ecosystem of the Antarctic, leopard seals survive by eating penguins. Penguins survive by eating a type of fish called krill. Krill depend on plankton, a type of seaweed, for food. Plankton, in turn, is affected by the amount of ultraviolet light from space. The amount of ultraviolet light is determined by the ozone layer.

The ozone layer is a shield around the earth that protects us from harmful ultraviolet rays. Because of human industry, there is a hole in the ozone. Because of this hole, there are not enough plankton for krill to eat. This means there are not enough krill for penguins to eat. Without enough penguins, the leopard seals do not have enough to eat. This is an example of one part of the ecosystem affecting all the other parts.

In the same manner, people depend on other organisms to live. If an imbalance occurs, people are also harmed. It is in everyone's best interest to protect endangered species. We also should prevent species not now in danger of extinction from becoming that way.

Plankton

Krill

Leopard
Seal

Penguin

The Ecosystem
of the Antarctic.

CHAPTER 4
What We Can Do

Most people don't kill black rhinoceros so they can make money by selling the rhinos' horns. Only a handful of people are killing gorillas to sell their hides. Few, if any of us, have given the order to destroy a million acres of tropical rainforest.

Even so, we all share the blame for the plight of endangered animals. We may not be doing anything directly to harm them, but by remaining silent, we are harming them all the same.

Helping endangered animals is easier than we might think. Here are a few things everyone can do to improve the future of **all** animals:

- Snip the plastic rings that come with six-packs of beverages. Seals, some of which already are endangered, can be killed if six-pack rings get around their necks. As the animals grow, the rings can choke them. Birds, turtles and other animals also die from trying to eat these rings.

- Buy pets such as cats, dogs, parakeets and hamsters. Avoid exotic pets such as macaws, cockatoos, monkeys, marmosets, pythons, boa constrictors and iguanas. The demand for these animals leads to the destruction of rainforests, and therefore, the reduction in habitat for many endangered animals.

- Don't buy products made of ivory, tortoiseshell, reptile skins, cat pelts or other products from endangered animals. Ask your family and friends to avoid purchasing these items, as well.

- Recycle paper, and use recycled paper whenever possible. Demand for paper leads to loss of habitat for animals when forests are cut down.

Did You Know . . .

Orioles love to eat oranges.

- Set up a bird feeder in your backyard.

- Join a wildlife organization such as the National Wildlife Federation, the World Wildlife Fund or the Natural Audubon Society.

- Don't buy products from tropical hardwoods such as teak, ebony, rosewood and mahogany. Demand for these products leads to the destruction of tropical rainforests, which destroys animal habitat. Ask your family and friends to avoid these items, too.

Did You Know . . .

Robins, Chickadees and Orioles like to use small lengths of string in their nests.

- Get your classmates involved in writing letters to encourage lawmakers to pass laws protecting endangered species.

Some Endangered Animals

Mountain gorilla
Mediterranean monk seal
Humpback whale
California condor
Whooping crane
Javan rhinoceros
Giant tortoise
Giant panda
Snow leopard
Yellow-footed rock wallaby
Lemur
Sea Turtle

A FINAL WORD

As human beings, we must realize that we share the earth with many creatures. As we use the earth's natural resources, we should keep in mind that other living organisms need those same resources, also. No one can change the wasteful habits of humans overnight. But by following the suggestions in this book, you can begin to make a difference in how we treat the animals of the earth.

GLOSSARY

ADAPT — To adjust to new conditions or surroundings.

DDT - A colorless, odorless poison that kills insects but also has a harmful effect on animals and birds.

ECOSYSTEM - The interaction of plants, animals and other natural elements surrounding an organism.

ENDANGERED - In danger of becoming extinct.

ENVIRONMENT - The surroundings in which a person, plant or animal lives.

EXTINCT - When a species of living things has died out and has completely disappeared from the earth.

HABITAT - The place where an animal or plant naturally lives and grows.

MAMMAL - A warm-blooded animal with a backbone. Most mammals are covered with fur or have some hair.

ORGANISM — A living plant or animal.

OZONE LAYER - The upper layer of the earth's atmosphere containing ozone gas that blocks out the sun's harmful ultaviolet rays.

POLLUTION - Harming the enivironment by putting man-made wastes in the air, water and ground.

PREHISTORIC - Belonging to a time before people started recording history.

RAINFOREST - A tropical woodland that receives 100 inches or more of rain a year.

REPRODUCE - To produce offspring.

SPECIES - A group of animals or plants that has certain characteristics in common.

INDEX